FLAME

BREWSTER GHISELIN

FLAME

University of Utah Press   Salt Lake City   1991

See Acknowledgments, page 43, for permission statements.

∞ The paper in this book meets the standards for
permanence and durability established by the
Committee on Production Guidelines for Book Longevity
of the Council on Library Resources

LIBRARY OF CONGRESS CATALOGING-IN-PUBLICATION DATA

Ghiselin, Brewster, 1903–
    Flame: poems, 1980–1990 / Brewster Ghiselin.
        p.   cm.
    Includes bibliographical references.
    ISBN 0-87480-371-3 (pbk.: alk. paper)
    I. Title.
PS3513.H5F57   1991
811'.54 — dc20   91-3583
                                               CIP

To OLIVE

CONTENTS

Appreciation of An Old Friend

by Allen Tate

In the summer of 1946 I first met Brewster Ghiselin. The occasion was a writers' conference at Logan, Utah. He was in early middle age, tall, distinguished, and so shy that one felt that the mere presence of a stranger, before the stranger had said anything beyond acknowledgment of our introduction, was profoundly disconcerting. This reticent poet had already suffered some twenty years of isolation and neglect; for, among his virtues as a man, there was and stiil is a rare innocence of motive: it has never occurred to Brewster Ghiselin, in the course of what is now a long life, that three-fourths of a literary reputation is the result of self-dramatization. For Ghiselin the total job of the poet is to write the poems, and then the poet withdraws.

I am not insinuating that he was not respected and admired by friends and colleagues in Utah. But there is always, for a poet in Utah, or Alabama, or Iowa, the Great World of Letters swarming in and around New York. The first man to read his poems from that World was the late John Peale Bishop, who was a close friend of mine, and from whom I first heard the name Brewster Ghiselin. But not until 1946 did I read and hear some of the work of this remarkable poet — a poet who resembles no other and whose diction and prosody are entirely his own, though highly traditional in a central Anglo-American tradition. Like all first-rate poets Brewster keeps his eye upon the work to be done: there is no effort towards originality — an effort that usually achieves only a commonplace eccentricity. A poet if he is original is not conscious of it. Ghiselin is that kind of poet. I consider his poem "Sea" one of the twentieth-century masterpieces. The Sea, the Wasatch Mountains, and the Desert have given him a wide and magnificent sweep of vision that no poet east of the Mississippi has achieved. In this quality he resembles (without being like) St.-John Perse. We have lived through a period of self-induced insanity among American poets. Brewster Ghiselin has serenely ignored this aberration; and he will last.

I must end this brief tribute to his poetry with a word about his personal integrity, his loyalty to his friends, and his selfless generosity. *November 25, 1971*

From *The Water of Light: A Miscellany in Honor of Brewster Ghiselin*, edited by Henry Taylor (Salt Lake City: University of Utah Press), 1976.

FLAME

TIDE

Away from ice under hover of cloud I have driven a thousand miles
Over mountains and snows, over deserts and the blasted lands
 and the gardens of our keeping,
Through cities in terrible hurtle of usual traffic (machines are not mad),
To come to this coast, homing through foreign land, home to the ocean,
Sea of Cortés where the whales and the gannets of the south
Are pelagic and the farther land
To the west is invisible as Thule,
And stars that were hidden are uncovered at evening over the sea.

I have watched them: and having slept I have come from the enclave
 of housing
Southward a little to the shore that is still unsold.

Inland across low dunes, the ebb is unheard;
Last flurries of terns crying over the lagoon have gone into landward light;
Under those green lush mangroves stilted in mud, on the farther shore,
The white of a noonday egret remains as it was.

On widening bars of brown sand in the fecund shallows, godwits and plovers
 and others of the birds of passage,
Too far and small for my naming,
Dabble and dip.

I am not alone. Far on the sheen of the narrows, under the southward
 mountains of cactus and cliff,
An oysterman, dark in the white of the boat, leans to the bird-white floats
 of his culture.

And here on the seaward dwindle of land,
Downstream where the tidal broth of draining estero quickens,

A man-long mummy that rode the shouldering flood some tides ago
Burdens the strand. Though gulls have taken the eyeballs, the leathery body
    is unbroached,
The teeth of the fisher, white pins in black blades of jaw, are uncovered to
    the curing sun.

A dolphin has come to the estero.

This shelf of grey shell underfoot
Crumples in dust of ash.

Salt on the wind,
Out of the swept west:

Over the wader's wave and the homeless foam.

GREEN WAVE OF CUYUTLAN

Dry strew of those dead small seasnakes, tatter and tangle trampled
Like cordage in powder of sand, measured a wave to come.
Ocean along that shore was tossing jostle of foam
Like cauldron calm that boils from walls of cataracts.
But none of those famous waves that darken and mound and mount
Far out from the April sand rose in that winter noon:
Nothing to show the force aflow of a green great wave
Gathering broad foam all up on to one long unflawed
Fluke curling flung to its fall over shorelings clambering ashore.

Only in turmoil and wrangle of shorelong deeps that are running
Always along the suck and stumble and drag of foams' end
The black of a bolebroad long log wallowing awash, diving:
Dancing a feast. A mouth in the thin water champing.
Leisurely and fast in shorestreams ferrying meat a slasher —
Shape of a tooth — swaying and lifting a blade of needs
Unsheathed yearlong in that place of the ola verde of April.

FLAME

That fish in the swim of haze over the city,
Sunsilvered fuselage slipping away to the east,
Sleek as a spike of ice in a stream speeding
Straight to the gleaming leap of a waterfall,
Flows to no finer goal than the gray ground,
To glide like a toy or fold its fins in flame.

Reading the future in no book of flame,
Seeing no gray but haze enfold our city,
Walking easy, though on ashen ground,
Breathing the bounty of the ambiguous East,
We count the nations slithering to their fall
On Fortune's hill or high on her wheel, speeding.

Leap of a shaft, twang of a string speeding
The shaft; then hands that tuned the twang; then flame
That fired the hand — then the black match, let fall.
Not out of the sky our furies sink to their city,
Nor swarm from our warded north, south, west, or east.
Nor rise up out of the sea or the underground.

Already with us, a long while, sure of their ground,
Breath of our breath, flesh of our flesh, speeding
On pleasure bent they please the gorgeous East
That holds the West in fee. On finless flame
They flaunt the mansions of a heavenly city,
They loft the flight of pride to no landfall.

Avid of fire they mount the last onfall,
Ready to rise and on predestined ground
Across the round of the world in a far city
Kindle a wick no treaties trim. Speeding
A long parade of flame to counter flame
They preach a western peace to the arming east.

God shield us! whirled on a great globe into the east
Like travelers lulled in a plane's lift and fall
Till they awake reading a scroll of flame —
Rescheduled, look to each other and the ground
And rise to take the ramp together, speeding
Ticketed for impact, into Fortune's city.

Far on the east and voiceless now to the ground
A plane is ranging away toward nightfall, speeding
To find a light, to circle a flame, a city.

THE DREAMERS

After a night of dreams
I am looking away,
southward over the Gulf,
and glad of my waking
freed of those versions of confusion,
trammels woven of ravel of memory and surmise,
I am reading
a measureless dawn,

the cat's-paws laid on the sea,
black birds crossing,
over the place of the catch,
dark men standing upright,
leaning, low in their boats
on the dawnlight,
lifting the gift of the waters,
fishermen, reading the nets.

ASHFALL

Easily we dream our deliverance: wilderness, air
Untainted by name,
Raven at rimrock,
Ocean before us

Or barrens bonesmooth of all but ash
The winds exalt,
Shroud lifted like lint whipt from the loom
Over the eyes
And into the idle
Hands no joy of consent
Upturns to receive it.

Easily we breathe a loftier vantage: heal-all
Of plotted paths,
Horizon walls,
Height more serene

Than Alhambra's that in fragrance of tuberose and rose
On its bastions of balconies
Looked to a lowland roaring dust
Over smoldering light
Of armies of deliverance
Coming to the parapet of gardens
Unready to receive them.

ALEXANDRIAN

Now as we fold up unread these pages
Crying the noon of the world's need, calling,
Blacker than cawing omens to deaf men,
Visionless eyes that tomorrow will lie with them
Heedless forever, though closer than lovers
Reading each other's lips in the dark
They sweeten with foreplay of speech, I am scanning
By ashlight, in augury, breathless embers.
I am tasting the savorless sweets of the dead.

LAGUNA BEACH: A CELEBRATION

Here, in the twenties, early,
where out of the sweep of the hills
a stream and a narrow road
came down to a scatter of houses
close to a clean, clear sea,
and islands lay on the west
daylong, on the clear days,
and later still
in the decade of the village changing,
in the decade of the town,
to the time of the city
climbing and clambering
that came with the peace of the world,
midcentury, over the land,
and the dark
ceased,
the lights
kindled at dusk
on shore and ocean
and no more
when the moon was down and the shorelong fog withdrawn to the edge of
    the west
the shore
looked at the stars nightlong
till the last of the stars strewn small in the end of night
were gone,
on the north and the south and the west
and over the sea-cold sand,
and the morning star from the east,
and day began
inviolate on the dawn's shore,
in the long forties of war
to wars' end,

still then
for a while
down the long coast
the cliffs stood bare,
the roofless reefs beyond in a float of foam,
the skylong leaning earth of inland hills lay clear,
the steep pastures greened
to a gleam of streams
out of rise on rise, wild over wild
tangle and stone upthrown and overthrown
to the pitch of a ridge,
slant grass
and tilt and topple of rock
rounded by sturdier stems in sungray leaves,
bristle of brush
where the walker shared the sky
with bushbirds, vultures, and hawks
and the coyote
stilled to watch.

THEFT

A writhe of gold on the highway in the night:
the headlights caught it but the wheels passed over
growling to stop on the gravelly shoulder, stopped,
the boxes along the trailer sizzling shock,
the cry of the driver, "Snake! Snake — get 'im!" I
running where the wheels had rolled, in a shadowy dazzle
on asphalt flashlit, hoping it gone alive
to the rock and the thickets, found it coiled — a jewel
fired by a sword of light: folds tightening fold
on fold, gold-flaked, fitted with emerald,
ring-gold on the floor of the dragon-hall of night.

Loosening my snakestick loop to pluck it up
I heard no step: no wakening stir but the nightwinds
near and far under the watch of stars.

TRIBUNAL

I
OILSPILL

. . . disaster? No,
not in the scope of ill stars.
Our bucket belly of riches
rips on a reef, tips and
grinds over snags, bumps and
is opening, racked in the tide
gushes libation, soils
the bridal bed of the world.

II
MAYDAY

Fearless of night,
the highway of stars,
the Plain of Wandering,
grief of Bellerophon
under the fallen
wing of law,
let us remember
pride of light,
thunder of liftoff,
trample of flame,
our lamp of law
trimmed in the White House,
suburb and city
luminous nightlong,
glitter of arc light
over a garden
of infinite privilege,
goal of the street people,

termless asphalt,
token of terror
under Olympus
cloistered in cloud.

III
<small>OFFERING</small>

Offer the apple of the Garden
to those who are hungry for life.
They take with delicate skepticism
of well-fed cats. They are thinking
of eagles, different delicacies,
fiery reward of wings,
as if they remembered desert
that bred the great bulls of Assyria
that Gaudier-Brzeska the sculptor
who died in the mud of war
dwarfed in his dream

EQUINOX

After the south,
Sirmione low in a rounding cling
of lakelight lapping
Rome,
and blossoming white in bare Desenzano
almonds
by windbreak walls
and sun-
green wavelets at morning slow
along rose-bisque moles
florid with ammonites curled in their sea of stone,

we rode the lake-edge north

away from noon
through towns of pleasure and summer
and past the last of the villas
and on along the bevel thrust of a mountain, slant
and more slant till steep
villages, orchards, and vineyards
ceased, and too deep for pier
sheer cliff
plumbed
and the road
blacked.

After the tunnels and the galleries,
the violet of the water
in windows of rock,
we rode by a gasp of waves,
between the black
generations of cypress,
the centuries of olives,
under the walls of winter:

ochre and brown and gray
lake-end steep as a fiord,
under Monte Rochetta.

The town was the winds'.

In a wedge of shade,
cold of the mountains of March,
furled walkers leaned,
boats came in at a gallop,
the tender long light whips of a willow
over a suck of gravel, of foam and trash,
leapt and lashed and streamed to the land —
and, beyond,
the long bright valley rose to the north,
the roads of war
to the passes under the snow.

Riva, in the cold spring — ice on the cliffs.

The sulfurous water of the Lago di Garda.

APOCALYPSE

Midocean
        only
its shifting gleams
tilting and lost

till out of that standing travel
gray under gray
              over black

a leap —   a leaper —   leaping
                        spindle of blue and brown
out of water
water to water
wave
     to wave
            a dolphin
another —   another —
                  and gone
and again
dolphin by dolphin
pied-sided

tandem and team
chariotless in harness of air

The People

alive in themselves and each other

moving in the grace of the sea
as in praise of the waters

of passage

       seaways

           waves

that reveal

to the pride
of the kindlers of fire

the delight of the dolphin.

FRAGMENT OF A DIALOGUE

for Gene England

Firm on our atoll, desert
Heart of bitter mirage,
Doubting believer, I stand with you
Sipping this brackish communion,
Breaking hard bread of alternatives —
Either a waste ocean
Or an infinite ocean of hope:
Whether these shimmering fronds
Above us, mere palms, are illusion,
Or else or also those petals,
That one Dove hovering descending
Out of the garden of the sun
To brood the hopes of humanity —
Both of such beautiful credentials,
Blazoned on measureless dark.

In terrible splendor of dilemma,
Saints walk into the night
To be washed of fire.
                    They return to us
Saying, "This shade is cool
Under the wings and the boughs.
Let us not forget one another."

ELEGY FOR JON

Between a stair and a stair
You died, alone,
Not between rock and rock
Half down the enormous drop of mountain cliff
Or on the ice-crest
You might have crossed,
Fearless, alone, that month
Of wilderness you dared,
For love of lonelier wild
Than most men love,
Height over height.

Between a stair and a stair.

Not as we feared
That afternoon you came
Hours late, when the mountain light
Had changed toward dusk,
While we waited,
Learning fear, counting your power of life
Against all doubt,
Until you came
Smiling out of the forest,
Treading the upland swale,
Blithe as a dancer
After the last pirouette
That made the tightrope hum.

LLEWELYN POWYS

Spring, 1929

I carrying your green tweed, of possible use,
through that cool afternoon we breathed above
the calm long west, blue-green Tyrrhenian sea,
we climbed a silent vineyard as if to a place
that might revolve in speech pleasure of two
that met as friends of friends, you at midlife,
I nearly as young as you were at my birth.

Little was said.

Years after, reading your praise of night and the sun,
a zebra mating — shot, that dappled cat
by a lake moonlit — shot at — vanished . . . till dawn
racked it earthlong, a hare at a tarn — drinking,
butterflies — flakes in the wind of their one summer,
I knew fivefold in proof a rule of grace,
silence, a perfect courtesy of breath.

THE IDLE POET TO THE BUSY EVANGELIST

A word never written
Is calling to be found,
Calling, crying
Like a lamb lost
Beyond the rockrim
Of the known land:

In country not imagined —
Wider than surmise,
Blinder than mist,
Like mist under foot —

A lost thing is luring
My flesh like a shepherd's
In fear and love
To the vast where it breathes
In the spell of the serpent,
In the arms of the sun.

ELEMENTAL

LABYRINTH

> Those who expect to find the clew within
> the walls never escape from them.
> — *Inscription assembled from fragments of*
> *plaster fallen in the ruins of Knossos.*

Noonday once more:
                    blaze of ocean
under this cliff
iron-red to its dip into air,
iron-brown
where caves of low tide
grind the long sprawl of their gravel,

and outward beyond the seabirds feeding
in shatter of seas over seas,
beyond the last foundering gleam
under sail-gray breath of whales,
beyond the farthest *palomas* folding and fanning foamwings that mingle
    with light,

that island
far and small
iron-black pivot of fire:

stub of a monolith lost to the clouds
yet held
in the vast of inference
whole,
iron-red, unspalled
term of a tract of dust preempting the sun,

still as the shaft of a gnomon over its scythe of shade,
hour after hour
over rubble of fallen fact
only the more as it was,
as it is, in the eye of insight
informing, appraising,
watching the walls
and the waste.

Vista — of a vision
like any, like all those others
unbreached forever: to look to,
to gaze away from,
far to that thread of cloud and beyond it
over the brown haze along the horizon,
that clew
ravelled along a path, whatever path or way,
in this place
of doorways and walls
we have made
to enclose us.

HAVEN

You looking away with the new-hacked stare of a figurehead scenting
    the sea wind
Over a necklace of foam,

You leaning away from your past like a hound
On a leash hurting the hand that holds it,

You at the limit of our light like a blind beak battering to be gone
From the cramp of the shell,

Listen:

> The lawns of summer
> Neighbor-leading mowers sweeten,
> Remembrance of fields
> And the night's meadows,
> Remembrance of silence after birdsong,
> Remembrance of silence
> Before there were birds.

The dragged drum of keel on shingle drawn by the trough,
Pull of foam and fog — no chart of landfall . . .

Nor hound's hearth . . .

Nor at last the nest
Of the everlasting arms.

No: only harsh wood of helm in hand like a helve,
Behind you the toppling bells and foamlike waving farewell
On the false trace of the wake the failed maps
Wandering, spreading and folding,
And before you
Halcyon storm.

GRANITE

A mountain pass: the highway stripped for our wheels,
Passing under between and around the pinnacled tumble of slopes,
Browned granite above, beside and below us,
Heap upon heap of the many accorded visitant eyes
Flying over them easily and fast like a season of birds,
Chaos of chance, as we say in our ignorance of all things, ourselves
    and our ambience,

At home with both, however we wander,
Looking for what is ours . . . finding . . .
Not finding:
As here on the highway climbing
The slant of a vaster pyramid than any of the boast of our kind,
The whole unappraisable mountain flowing away like sand,
A cairn of silences cemented by the eloquence of unanswerable questions.

PELAGIC

> ". . . a few birds screamed on motionless wings
> over the swaying mastheads.
> But soon the land disappeared,
> the birds went away . . ."
> — *Joseph Conrad*

Moving — not like the gulls
in the busy wake of a ship,
more like the gannets

crossing the farthest intent of prows,
over the wake of a wave they skim
to their goal of air,

over the foam of no prow,
white pour of the wind;

moving — not like the winds —
to the goal of breath,

a wider wild than the grove of the leaf
that flies home to the hands of a ship,
in the beak of a dove.

HERE

Trivia — three-roads, crossroads:
the passing show and shuffle of things,
inpouring and pouring away;
the three
faces of a god,
offering choice: viaticum . . . .
Come,
with me.
You shall
(not)
be saved. Or:
I am the way, all ways together, all three,
or as in a city, a radiant
show of escape — at the point of convergence,
the heart of the plan,
the center,
the point of departure.

PRISONS

for Giovanni Battista Piranesi

Burials: The brutal lines
Of thoughtful poems,
Too much salt,
Fixations.

Carceri:
Infinite speculation,
Endless chains
Of intellectual deliverance.

Careful! You can misread this,
Reading as always
To savor — simply —
The death in it.

Truth!
How sweet it is,
Breathed in the forest of illusion,
The scent of the forest.

VIGIL

The mountains are falling.

And the foot of my love — or yours, or another's —
In dew-cold night, before dawn,
Is touching a dusty path.

OF WINGS

for Olive, with my gift of O TO BE A DRAGON, 1959

O to flutter away on
reptilian carnation
    petal fans
             (in fours!) —
   Marianne's
            (of course) :
   O shun man's
lesser imagination
           (for Moore's).

PETREL

Who shall praise completeness and not be caught in it?

"I," said the petrel laying the palmate leaf
Of light foot on the wave. "My footsteps fling
The withering seas — the whole of ocean — down.
My wingwinds speed the storms that fly with me
Across the prows the dolphins lead astray."

THE WELL-BELOVED

Neat as a whippet
But doll-size, dolldog
Flibbertigibbet,
Off for his morning
Walk, goosesteps
At both ends.
Jaunty in ears
And piglet twist,
He skips, steps,
Stops, savoring
Under his forepaws
In ashen grass
This — that, sniffets.
Squanders, in a minute,
Hours. Wiggling
Gallop banishes
Cat. He snicks
Up snow for a sherbet.
Preoccupations
Of men and nations
Are not his: what
Is, he looks to.

SEMBLANCE ON SEMBLANCE

Stone-white between the wings and along the arc of wing and wing,
the primaries black of stone, in the sun over water of morning,
high
pelicans turn, curve upon curve unfalling

till flicker and dip and twist — as if
wingbone broke —
topple and drop

beak into sea.

Foam of that fall
flowers like a bush.

Black root stript of boughs
in a strew of flowers
rounds and writhes,

a boulder swims,

beast-back humped on the kill
in the withering foam
flings up long like an angel's — stone-grey — wings that fell.

RAIN IN AUTUMN

The tobacco trees shake all the rain from themselves,
and hang again,
subtly gathering rain.
                    Rain!
and the fine sky like a sleep, drifting down,
finely particled, perfectly distributed:
this autumn rain is like sleep,
so gently, without emphasis it falls.

Grey-litten space, the crouched land low and silent under a height
that is like forgetting,
resolved and separate, the upper rain, and the air

THE INFINITE

This lonely hill has been dear to me always,
and this hedge, that is hiding so long
a reach of horizon. But now,
as I sit here gazing, interminable
spaces beyond it, and silences transcending
man, and deepest quiet
brim in my mind, almost with fear.
And as I listen to the wind
swirling its green speech amid leaves
I compare that infinite silence
to this voice: I remember eternity,
and the dead seasons, and the present and living
time, and the sound of it.
So lost in this vast my thought drowns:
and shipwreck is sweet in this sea.

Giacomo Leopardi
L'infinito,
translation by
Brewster Ghiselin

FRAGMENT

A sword,
A sword of iron forged in cold of dawn,
A sword with runes
None can be deaf to nor clearly decipher,
A sword of the Baltic that will be sung in Northumbria,
A sword the poets
Will beat to the temper of ice and fire,
A sword a king will give to a king
And this king to a dream,
A sword that will be true
To an hour that Destiny knows,
A sword for the light of battle.

A sword for the hand
That will rule the beautiful battle, the tissue of men,
A sword for the hand
That will redden the fangs of the wolf
And the pick of the pitiless raven,
A sword for the hand
That will squander red gold,
A sword for the hand
That will topple the dragon to sleep on his bed of gold,
A sword for the hand
That will conquer a kingdom and lose a kingdom,
A sword for the hand
That will fell the forest of spears,
A sword for the hand of Beowulf.

Jorge Luis Borges
Fragmento,
translation by
Brewster Ghiselin.

CIAO

they signal
high
in the sunset
over the Arno
the bats
aflitter
like little
black gloves
goodby
hello
and goodby

*Translation by
Brewster Ghiselin*

CIAO

segnalano
in alto
nel tramonto
sopra l'Arno
i pipistrelli
guizzando
come piccoli
guanti neri
arrivederci
arrivederci
e addio

LEONE TRAVERSO

Caro
mi' amico,
adesso
siamo in Firenze,

ancora

nell'oro
della tavola ampia
d'amicizia,

la voce generosa
dicendo lentamente,
in inglese,
"*Ghi*-se-lin,
*Gee*zayleen —
what a *pretty* name . . ."

ed io
istantemente
cambiato in italiano . . .

per poco, un momento, un'ora:
pane e vino —

e dopo
nella sera formicolante
delle strade striate di neri e lumi
siamo partiti
nel buio e rumore
degli anni.

LEONE TRAVERSO

Dear friend,
now
we are in Florence,

again

in the gold
amplitude of the table
of friendship,

your generous voice
outpouring
slowly
your English,
"*Ghi*-se-lin,
Geezayleen —
what a *pretty* name . . ."

and I
instantly
an Italian . . .

for a while, a moment, an hour:
bread and wine —

and afterward
at evening in swarming
streets striped with blacks and with lights
we turned from each other
to the darkness and uproar
of the years.

Translation by
Brewster Ghiselin

HONOR AND HONORS

Now fear them — loud hounds
That lifelong fearless you outran:
They are fawning to lick your hand.

OSPREY

The fishhawk on the cactus —
There the fishhawk sat
Silent in the silent sun —
Stroked his bloody beak,
Gazed into the pathless light.

ACKNOWLEDGMENTS

The author and publisher thank the following periodicals:

Letteratura, for "Ciao," the original Italian version (Maggio-Giugno 1968)

Literature and Belief, for "Fragment of a Dialogue," (1986)

Michigan Quarterly Review, for "Fragment," (Fall 1972)

Palaemon Press Broadside series, for "The Dreamers," (1981)

Poetry, for "Equinox," "Apocalypse," (March 1980); "Semblance on Semblance," "Theft," (February 1981); "Flame," "The Well-Beloved," "Green Wave of Cuyutlan," (March 1983); "Honor and Honors," (April 1988)

Quarterly West, for "Alexandrian," (Fall / Winter 1985); "ELEMENTAL," a sequence comprising the poems "Labyrinth," "Haven," "Granite," "Pelagic," "Here," "Prisons," "Vigil," (10th Anniversary Issue, 1986)

Western Humanities Review, for "The Infinite," (Winter 1973)

Willow Springs, for "Leone Traverso" (the original Italian and the translation), "Llewelyn Powys," "A Celebration," retitled "Laguna Beach: A Celebration," (Winter 1986)

The translation of "Fragmento" is printed by permission of Jorge Luis Borges and the Delacorte Press, publisher of Borges' *Poems: 1923–1967*. Edited with an Introduction and Notes by Norman Thomas di Giovanni, 1971.